THE DATA

Deep Learning Pocket Reference Guide

A quick pocket reference guide to a collection of deep learning algorithms and key terms

TABLE OF CONTENTS

Preface

Deep Learning Pocket Reference guide walks you through a collection of the most important deep learning algorithms, key concepts, and terminologies.

This book can be used for quickly learning, revising, and recapping deep learning concepts. This book can be used as a quick reference guide to prepare for deep learning interviews. You will learn and revise deep learning algorithms like artificial neural networks, recurrent neural networks, convolutional neural networks, generative adversarial neural networks. You will also look into concepts like weight initialization, batch normalization, drop out, learning rate scheduling, and many others.

This quick reference guide to deep learning will help you to revise the deep learning concepts with pleasing animated characters. With this deep learning pocket reference guide, you can revise the algorithms anytime and anywhere you are.

Fundamentals
of
Deep
Learning

Deep Neural Network

The artificial neural network consists of one input, N number of hidden and one output layer. When the artificial neural network consists of a large number of hidden layers then it is often called the deep neural network.

Transfer Function

The transfer function is most commonly known as the activation function. It is mainly used for establishing non-linearity in the neural network.

That is, it is mainly used for introducing the non-linear transformation in the neural network for learning the intricate patterns in the data.

Sigmoid vs Tanh Function

The sigmoid activation function scales the value between 0 to 1 and it is centered at 0.5 whereas the tanh activation function scaled the value between -1 to 1 and it is centered at 0.

Dying ReLU Problem

Suppose, x is given as an input to the ReLU function. If the value of x is less than 0 then the ReLU function returns 0 as output.

If the value of x is greater than or equal to 0 then the ReLU function returns x as output. Thus, the ReLU function always returns 0 when the value of x is less than 0 (that is, when x is a negative value) and this is often referred to as the dying ReLU problem.

Combating Dying ReLU Problem

To combat the dying ReLu problem, we use the Leaky ReLU. With the leaky ReLU activation function, we introduce a small slope for a negative value.

That is, instead of always returning the 0 every time when x is a negative value, leaky ReLU returns the x multiplied by a small number called alpha. We usually set the value of alpha to 0.01.Thus, leaky ReLU returns x when x is greater than or equal to 0 and it returns x multiplied by alpha when x is less than 0.

Parametric ReLU vs Randomized ReLU

In the leaky ReLU, instead of setting the alpha to a small value, we can feed the alpha as a parameter to the network and let the network learn the optimal value of the alpha and this type of leaky ReLU is often called the parametric ReLU function.

In the leaky ReLU, we can also set the random value to the alpha. When the value of alpha is set to some random value it is often called the randomized ReLU function.

Why Softmax function in Output layer?

The softmax function converts the given inputs to the range of 0 to 1. It acts as a generalization of the sigmoid activation function.

When we perform a classification task, it is more desirable to apply the softmax function in the output layer since it returns the probability of each class being the output.

Epochs vs Iteration

One iteration implies that our network has seen a batch of data points once whereas one epoch implies that our network has seen all the data points once.

Neurons in Input and Output Layer

The number of neurons in the input layer is set to the number of inputs. The number of neurons in the output layer is set based on the task we perform.

For instance, if we are performing regression, then we can set the number of neurons in the output layer to 1. If we are performing classification, then we can set the number of neurons in the output layer to a number of classes present in the dataset where each neuron emits the probability of the corresponding class being an output.

Neurons in Hidden Layer

The number of neurons in the hidden layer can be set based on any of the following methods:

The number of hidden neurons should be between the size of the input layer and the size of the output layer.

The number of hidden neurons should be 2/3 the size of the input layer, plus the size of the output layer.

The number of hidden neurons should be less than twice the size of the input layer

Number of Hidden Layers

There is not any standard and optimal way to decide the number of hidden layers. We can choose the number of hidden layers based on the intuitiveness obtained from the problem we are dealing with.

For a simple problem, we can build the network with 2 or less than 2 hidden layers and for a complex problem, we can build a deep network with many hidden layers. As specified earlier, there is no rule of thumb in deciding the number of hidden layers.

Dropout

Dropout often referred to the dropping off some of the neurons in the neural network.

That is, while training the network we can ignore certain neurons randomly and this helps is preventing the network from overfitting to the training data.

Early Stopping

Early stopping is often used to control overfitting. With early stopping, we stop the process of training the neural network before the weights have converged.

That is, we check the performance of our network on the validation set which is not used for the training. When the performance of the network has not been improved over the validation set then we stop training the network.

Internal Covariate Shift

While training the deep network, the distribution of the hidden units activation value changes due to the change in weights and bias. This leads to the problem called the internal covariate shift and causes the training time to slow down. We can avoid this problem of internal covariate shift by applying batch normalization.

Batch normalization as the name suggests denotes the normalizing hidden units activation value. It also helps in reducing the training time of the network.

Data Augmentation

Data augmentation is widely used for increasing training data. Suppose, we are training the network to perform an image classification task and we have only less number of images in our training set and we have no access to obtain more images to include in the training set.

In that case, we can perform data augmentation by cropping, flipping, and padding the images and obtain the new images and include them in our training set.

Data Normalization

Data normalization is usually performed as a preprocessing step. Data normalization implies we normalize the data points by subtracting the mean of each data point and dividing by its standard deviation.

It helps in attaining better convergence during training the network.

Initializing Zero Weights

It is not a good practice to initialize all the weights with zero. During backpropagation, we train the network by calculating the gradients of the loss function with respect to the weights.

When we set all the weights to zero, then the derivatives will have the same value for all the weights. This makes the neurons to learn the same feature. Thus, when we set all the weights to zero, then we end up with a network where all the neurons learn the same feature.

Weight Initialization Methods

Some of the most commonly used weight initialization methods include random initialization and Xavier initialization.

Hyperpara-meters of Neural Network

Some of the hyperparameters of the network include the following:

Number of neurons in the hidden layer
Number of hidden layers
The activation function in each layer
Weight initialization
Learning rate
Number of epochs
Batch size

Training Deep network

We train the network by performing backpropagation. During backpropagation, we apply any optimization method and find the optimal weights.

Gradient descent is the most commonly used optimization method while training the network during backpropagation.

Preventing Overfitting in Deep Neural Networks

Some of the methods used for preventing overfitting in neural networks include the following:

Dropouts
Early stopping
Regularization
Data augmentation

Gradient Descent Methods

Gradient Descent

Gradient descent is the most popular and widely used optimization algorithms used for training neural networks.

Gradient descent is the first-order optimization method because with gradient descent we calculate only the first-order derivative.

Working of Gradient Descent

Gradient descent is an optimization method used for training the network.

First, we compute the derivatives of the loss function with respect to the weights of the network and then update the weights of the network using the below update rule:

Weight = weight - learning rate x derivatives

Jacobian Matrix

The matrix is often called the Jacobian matrix if it contains the first-order partial derivatives.

Small and Large Learning Rate

When the learning rate is small then we take a very small step and it slows down attaining the convergence and when the learning rate is large then we take a very large step and it may cause us to miss out on the global minimum.

Gradient Checking

Gradient checking is used for debugging the gradient descent algorithm and to make sure that we have a correct implementation.

That is, when we implement the gradient descent method for the complex neural network, even with buggy implementations, the network will learn something.

But the buggy implementation will not be as optimal as a bug-free implementation. So to ensure that we have the bug free implementation of gradient descent we perform gradient checking.

Analytical and Numerical Gradients

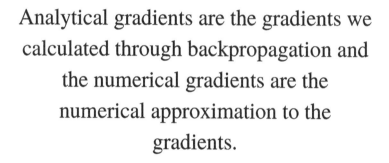

Analytical gradients are the gradients we calculated through backpropagation and the numerical gradients are the numerical approximation to the gradients.

Gradient Checking

In gradient checking, first, we compute the analytical and approximated numerical gradients. Then we compare the analytical and numerical gradients. If they are not the same then there is an error with our implementation.

We don't have to check whether analytical and numerical gradients are exactly the same since the numerical gradient is just an approximation. So, we compute the difference between the analytical and numerical gradients and if their difference is very small say 1e-7 then our implementation is correct else we have a buggy implementation.

Convex and Non-Convex Function

A function is called a convex function when it has only one minimum value and a function is called a non-convex function when it has more than one minimum value.

Need of Stochastic Gradient Descent

With gradient descent, we update the parameters of the model only after iterating through all data points present in our training set. Let's say we have 10 million data points.

Now, even to perform a single parameter update, we have to iterate through all the 10 million data points and then we update the parameter of the network. This is will be a very time-consuming task and takes us a lot of training time. So, to combat this drawback of gradient descent, we can stochastic gradient descent.

Stochastic Gradient Descent

With stochastic gradient descent, we don't have to update the parameters of the network only after iterating through all data points present in our training set.

Instead, we can update the parameter of the network after iterating through every single point in the training set.

Mini-Batch Gradient Descent

With the mini-batch gradient descent, we don't update the parameters of the network after iterating through every single data point in our training set.

Instead, we update the parameters of the network after iterating through some n number of points. Say n is 32, then it implies that we update the parameter of the network after iterating through every 32 data points in our training set.

Different Gradient Descent Methods

Gradient descent - Update the parameters of the network after iterating through all the data points present in the training set.

Stochastic gradient descent - Update the parameter of the network after iterating through every single data points present in the training set.

Mini-batch gradient descent - Update the parameter of the network after iterating through some n number of data points present in the training set

Momentum Based Gradient descent

One problem we face with SGD and mini-batch gradient descent is that there will be too many oscillations in the gradient steps. This oscillation happens because we update the parameter of the network after iterating through every point or every n data points and thus the direction of the update will possess some variances causing oscillation in the gradient steps.

This oscillation leads to slow training time and makes it hard to reach the convergence. To avoid this issue we use momentum-based gradient descent.

Issues Faced in the Momentum Based Gradient descent

One issue we encounter with the momentum-based gradient descent method is that it causes to miss out the minimum value.

Suppose, we are near to attaining convergence and when the value of momentum is high, then the momentum pushes the gradient step high and we miss out on the minimum value, that is we overshoot the minimum value.

Nesterov Accelerated Momentum

Nesterov accelerated momentum is used to solve the issue faced with the momentum-based method. With the Nesterov accelerated momentum, we calculate gradients at the lookahead position, instead of calculating gradient at the current position.

The lookahead position implies the position where the momentum would take us to.

Adaptive Methods of Gradient Descent

Adaptive methods of gradient descent include the following:

Adagrad
Adadelta
RMSProp
Adam
Adamax
AMSGrad
Nadam

Setting Learning Rate Adaptively

We can set the learning rate adaptively using adagrad. Using adagrad method, we assign a high learning rate when the previous gradient value is low and we assign a low learning rate when the previous gradient value is high.

This makes the learning rate to change adaptively based on the past gradient updates.

Adam Optimizer VS RMSProp

In Adam, we compute the running average of squared gradients as we compute in RMSProp.

But instead of computing only the running average of squared gradients, we also compute the running average of gradients, That is, Adam uses both first and second moments of the gradients.

AMSGrad

Due to the exponentially moving the average of gradients, Adam fails to reach convergence and may reach the sub-optimal solution instead of the globally optimal solution.

This happens because when we use the exponentially moving average of gradients, we miss the information about the gradients that occur less frequently. So, to combat this issue, we use AMSGrad.

Convolutional Neural Networks

Why CNN for Image data?

The convolutional neural network uses the special operation called convolution which is capable of extracting important features from the image.

Since the convolutional operation extracts good features from the image, the accuracy of CNN is high compared to the other algorithms for the image data.

Different Layers Used in CNN

The convolutional neural network uses the following three important layers:

Convolutional layer
Pooling layer
Fully connected layer

Convolution Operation

We take the input matrix and one more matrix called the filter matrix.

We slide the filter matrix over the input matrix by n number of pixels, perform element-wise multiplication, sum up the results and produce a single number and this operation is known as convolution.

Activation Maps

The matrix obtained as a result of convolution operation is often called activation maps or feature maps.

Stride

In the convolution operation, we take the filter matrix and slide it over the input matrix by n number of pixels, perform element-wise multiplication, sum the result and produce a single number.

The number of pixels we choose to slide the filter matrix over the input matrix is often called the stride

Value of Stride

If we set stride to a high value, then it takes us less time to compute but we might miss out on some important feature from the image.

If we set stride to a low value, then we can learn the more detailed representation fo the image but it will take us a lot of time to compute.

Padding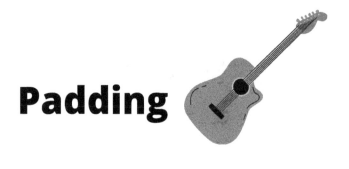

When we slide the filter matrix over the input matrix, in some cases, the filter matrix does not fit the input matrix perfectly, when the filter matrix does not fit the input matrix perfectly we apply padding.

Same Padding
VS
Valid Padding

When we pad the input matrix with zero values is called same padding and instead of padding if we discard the region of input matrix which does not fit well with the input matrix then it is called valid padding.

Need of Pooling Layers

The activation map which is obtained as a result of the convolutional operation will have a large dimension. To reduce the dimension of activation maps, we use the pooling layer.

Different Types of Pooling

The different types of pooling include the following:

Max pooling
Average pooling
Sum pooling

Working of CNN

Let's say we performing an image classification task. First, we feed the image as input to the network and perform the convolution operation.

The convolution operation extracts the important features from the image and produces the feature map. Then we feed this feature map to the fully connected layer which performs the classification task.

Architecture
of
VGG Net

The architecture of VGG consists of convolutional layers followed by a pooling layer. VGG net uses 3 x 3 convolution and 2 x 2 pooling.

It is often referred to as VGG-n and the n corresponds to a number of layers, excluding the pooling and softmax layer.

Use of Multiple Filters in Inception Network

Let's suppose we are performing an object detection task. The object can appear anywhere in the image. That is, the object can be in the center region of the image, or it can be in the small corner of the image. Also, the shape of the object can vary from image to image.

In some images, the object takes large shape while in other images the object takes small shape. Since the object in the image varies greatly in the image in terms of size and location, it is difficult to identify the object in the image if we use only a single filter with a fixed size. So in the inception network, we use multiple filters of varying sizes.

Inception Blocks in Inception Network

The inception network contains nine inception blocks. These nine inception blocks are stacked one above the other.

First, we take the input image and we perform the convolutional operation with three filters of varying size which includes 1 x 1, 3 x3, and 5 x5. Then we feed the result of the convolutional operation to the next inception block.

1 x 1 Convolution

1x1 convolution implies that we use one filter of size 1 x 1.

It is widely used for reducing the number of depth channels.

Factorized Convolution

We can break down a convolutional layer with a larger filter size into a stack of convolutional layers with smaller filter size and this is known as factorized convolution.

Suppose, we have a convolutional layer with a 5 x 5 filter then it can be broken down into two convolutional layers with 3 x 3 filters.

LeNet Architecture

The LeNet architecture consists of seven layers as given below:

Three convolutional layers
Two pooling layers
One fully connected layer
One output layer

Drawbacks of CNN

CNN is translation-invariant and this makes CNN more prone to misclassification.

Say, for instance, we are performing a face recognition task then CNN checks only the presence of facial features such as eyes, nose, mouth, and ears. It will not check whether those features are present in the correct locations.

If the images have all those features then it will be classified as the face irrespective of the location of the features. This is one of the major drawbacks of CNN.

Recurrent Neural Networks

RNN VS FNN

In the recurrent neural network, to predict the output, instead of using only the current input we also use the previous hidden state.

The previous hidden state holds the information about what the network has seen so far whereas in the feedforward network, to predict the output, we use only the current input.

Vanishing Gradient Problem

Suppose, we initialize the weights of the network randomly with small values. During backpropagation, we compute the derivative of the hidden layer and multiply them by weights at every step while moving backward.

This derivative and weights, both of which are a small number. When we multiply two numbers which are small then the result will be a smaller number. So, when we multiply the weights and derivative at every step then our gradient becomes an infinitesimally small number and this is called vanishing gradient problem.

Preventing Vanishing Gradient Problem

We can prevent the vanishing gradient problem by using the ReLu activation function instead of tanh or sigmoid activation. We can also avoid vanishing gradient problem by using a variant of RNN called LSTM.

Preventing Exploding Gradient Problem

We can prevent the exploding gradient problem by using gradient clipping. With the gradient clipping method, we normalize the gradients according to an L2 norm and clip the gradient value to a specific range.

Using RNN Over FNN

The recurrent network is preferred over feedforward networks when we want to perform a sequential tasks.

Since the recurrent neural network store the past information in the hidden state, the recurrent neural network is very effective for a sequential tasks than the feedforward network.

LSTM VS RNN

LSTM differs from RNN by introducing three special gates called input gate, forget gate and output gate.

Cell and Hidden State in LSTM

In LSTM, the cell state is mainly used for storing the information and it is also referred to as the internal memory whereas the hidden state is mainly used for computing the output.

Bidirectional RNN VS Vanilla RNN

Unlike Vanilla RNN, bidirectional RNN is used for reading the inputs in both directions. It consists of two different layers of hidden units.

In one layer, the hidden states are shared from left to right, and in the other layer, they are shared from right to left and both of these layers connect from the input layer to the output layer.

Seq2Seq Model

The sequence-to-sequence model (seq2seq) is the many-to-many RNN architecture.

It is widely used in various applications where we need to map an arbitrary-length input sequence to an arbitrary-length output sequence. The example includes music generation, chatbots and more.

Generative
Adversarial
Networks

Discriminative VS Generative Models

The discriminative model classifies the data points into their respective classes by learning the decision boundary that separates the classes in an optimal way.

The generative models can also classify the data points, however, instead of learning the decision boundary, they learn the characteristics of each of the classes.

GANs and Implicit Density Model

The generator network generates new data points similar to the ones present in the training set. In order to generate a new data point, the generator implicitly learns the distribution of the training set and based on this implicitly learned distribution the generator generates the new data point.

Since the generator network implicitly learns the distribution of the training set, GANs are often called the implicit density model

Generator
VS
Discriminator

The role of the generator is to generate new data points that are similar to the ones present in the training set.

The role of the discriminator is to classify the given data points as to whether it is a real data point or it is generated by the generator.

DCGAN

GANs are widely used in applications which involve image such as image generation, converting grayscale image to colored image and so on. When dealing with images, we use CNN instead of a feed-forward neural network since CNN is effective at handling images.

Similarly, instead of using vanilla GAN, we can use DCGAN whose generator and discriminator involve the convnets instead of the feed-forward networks. The DCGAN is very effective at tasks related to the images than the vanilla GANs.

Generator of DCGAN

The generator of the DCGAN consists of the convolutional transpose and batchnorm layers with ReLU activations.First, we draw a noise from a normal distribution and feed that as an input to the generator.

The generator which is composed of convolutional transpose and batch norm layers takes this noise as an input and generates an image similar to the ones present in the training set.

Discriminator
of
DCGAN

The discriminator of DCGAN consists of series of convolutional and batch norm layers with leaky ReLU activations.

First, we take the image and feed the image as an input to the discriminator, then the discriminator performs a series of convolution operation and then classifies whether the image is a fake image generated by the generator or the image is a real image from the training data.

Least Square GAN

In the GAN, we use sigmoid cross-entropy as the loss function. The problem with the sigmoid cross-entropy loss is that once the fake samples are on the correct side of the decision surface, then gradients tend to vanish even though the fake samples are far away from the true distribution.

To avoid this issue we use the least-squares GAN. In the least-squares GAN, although the fake samples generated by the generator are on the correct side of the decision surface, gradients will not vanish until the fake samples match the true distribution.

Wasserstein GAN

In GAN, we minimize the JS divergence between the generator distribution and the real data distribution. But the problem with the JS divergence is that it is not applicable when there is no overlap or when the two distributions do not share the same support.

So, to avoid this issue, we can use the Wasserstein GAN which uses the Wasserstein distance instead of JS divergence.

Wasserstein Distance

The Wasserstein distance is also commonly known as the Earth Movers (EM) distance.

It is used as the distance measure in the optimal transport problems where we need to move things from one configuration to another.

Conditional GAN

With the vanilla GAN, we cannot control and modify the images generated by the generator of the GAN. So, we use conditional GAN.

With conditional GAN, we can control and modify the images generated by the generator of the GAN.

InfoGAN

We can perceive InfoGAN as an unsupervised version of conditional GAN.

In the conditional GAN, we impose a condition on the generator and discriminator to generate the image we want based on the class labels present in the dataset.

When we have the unlabelled dataset then we can use InfoGAN for generating the images we want.

CycleGAN

The CycleGAN maps the data from one domain to another domain.

That is, in the CycleGAN, we map the distribution of images from one domain to the distribution of images in another domain.

Applications of CycleGAN

CycleGAN is majorly used in the premises where it is difficult to obtain the paired training samples.

Some of the interesting applications of CycleGAN include:

Photo enhancement
Season transfer
Converting the real pictures to the artistic pictures and so on.

Cycle Consistent Loss

In the Cycle GAN, the generator map the images from the source domain to a random permutation of images in the target domain which can match the target distribution.

So, to alleviate this, we use a special type of loss called cycle consistent loss.

StackGAN

We can generate images just based on the text using an interesting type of GAN called StackGAN.

The StackGAN works in two stages:

In the first stage, they generate a basic outline, primitive shapes, and create a low-resolution version of the image.

In the second stage, they enhance the picture generated in the first stage by making it more realistic and then convert them into a high-resolution image.

Autoencoders

Autoencoders
VS
PCA

The difference between the autoencoder and PCA is that PCA uses linear transformation for dimensionality reduction while the autoencoder uses a nonlinear transformation for dimensionality reduction.

Bottleneck

The autoencoders map the data of a high dimension data to a low-level representation. This low-level representation of data is called as latent representation or bottleneck.

The bottleneck comprises of only meaningful and important features that represent the input.

Encoder and Decoder

The encoder takes the given input and outputs the low dimensional latent representation of the input. The decoder takes this low dimensional latent representation generated by the encoder as an input and tries to reconstruct the original input.

Overcomplete vs Uncercomplete Autoencoder

When the code or latent representation has the dimension higher than the dimension of the input then the autoencoder is called the overcomplete autoencoder.

On the contrary, when the code or latent representation has the dimension lower than the dimension of the input then the autoencoder is called the Undercomplete autoencoder.

Working of Convolutional autoencoders

We feed the input image to the encoder which consists of a convolutional layer. The convolutional layer performs the convolution operation and extracts important features from the image.Next, we apply the max pooling operation to retain only the important features of the image and obtain a latent representation of the image, called a bottleneck.

To the decoder, we feed the bottleneck as an input. The decoder consists of deconvolutional layers and it performs the deconvolution operation and tries to reconstruct the image from the bottleneck.

Sparse Autoencoder

When we set many nodes in the hidden layer then we can learn better and robust latent representation of the input. But the problem is when we keep more nodes in the hidden layer, then the autoencoders overfit the training data.

To combat this problem of overfitting, we need a sparse autoencoder.

Sparse
Constraint

The sparse autoencoder introduces a special constraint in the loss function called a sparse constraint.

The sparse constraint is used to make sure that the autoencoder is not overfitting to the training data when we set the many nodes in the hidden layer.

Contractive Autoencoders

In order to make sure that our encodings are more robust to small perturbations present in the training set, we use the contractive autoencoders.

The contractive autoencoders use a new penalty term in the loss function which penalizes the representations that are too sensitive to the input.

Embedding based methods

Word Embeddings

Word embeddings are the vector representations of words in a vector space.

Use of Word Embedding

The word embeddings capture the syntactic and semantic meanings of a word which helps our network to understand the word better.

CBOW vs Skipgram model

In the CBOW model, the goal of the network is to predict a target word given its surrounding words whereas, in the skip-gram model, the goal of the network is to predict surrounding words given a target word.

Evaluating Embedding

We can evaluate embedding by the following:

Performing word similarity, Projecting them to the embedding space
Visualization
Clustering

Paragraph Vector

The paragraph vector learns the vector representation of the whole paragraph thus capturing the subject of the paragraph.

TensorFlow

DataFlow Graphs

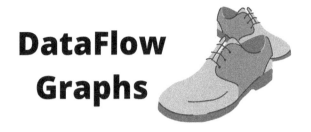

Every computation in TensorFlow is represented by a graph called data flow graph or computational graph.

It consists of several nodes and edges, where nodes are mathematical operations, such as addition and multiplication, and edges are tensors.

Running DataFlow Graphs

In order to run the data flow graph, we use a TensorFlow session.

Creating TensorFlow Session

TensorFlow sessions can be created as tf.Session()

Variables
vs
Placeholders

We use the variables for storing the values. Variables are used as input to several other operations in a computational graph.

We can think of placeholders as variables, where we only define the type and dimension, but do not assign the value. Values for the placeholders will be fed at runtime.

The feed_dict Parameter

The feed_dict parameter is the dictionary where the key represents the name of the placeholder and the value represents the value of the placeholder.

Eager Execution

Eager execution in TensorFlow allows for rapid prototyping.

The eager execution follows the imperative programming paradigm, where any operations can be performed immediately, without having to create a graph.

TensorFlow Serving

As mentioned in the tensorflow documentation, TensorFlow Serving is a flexible, high-performance serving system for machine learning models, designed for production environments. TensorFlow Serving makes it easy to deploy new algorithms and experiments while keeping the same server architecture and APIs. TensorFlow Serving provides out-of-the-box integration with TensorFlow models but can be easily extended to serve other types of models and data.